ALL THESE HANDS ARE TREE TRUNKS

GARRETT SHERWOOD

Copyright © 2014 Garrett Sherwood

All rights reserved.

Don't steal my stuff.

Cover Art by Drew Grella
drewdrawing.tumblr.com

DEDICATION

This book is essentially a story of how I found my way to her,
the her,
so it would be silly to dedicate it to anyone else.

To Brittany.

Contents

you cannot eat poems	9
pamplona	13
then you'd drown	14
it's like I said	16
they tell me the earth is tilted	17
badlands and cornfields	18
this is what I think of sailboatin	23
big bopper	24
honestly	26
leopold	27
1967 RV(green)(with the windows down)	31
the next time I kiss you	32
soft directions	33
three	35
corruptible	36
a lesson in cosmic love connections	39
jolly baba	40
for keeps	44
dancing	49

little girl	50
the day she moved away	51
this right is not always	52
the girl who always sat by the window	55
the bug catcher	56
bathtub poems	59
I write about these people	61
big empty house	62
on our way to portland	67
baldassare	69
idaho	72
in this book	73
the middle	75
while the faucet is running	76
why tiresmashed squirrels are not squirrels	78
the things I would tell him	80
when the cynic gets happy he drives faster	87
I saw a ghost today	88
church of chainsaw silence	89
chloe	92
in the dark	94
strawberry moon	95
one thousand miles per hour	100

the hunt	104
alan and me	105
february 15th club for non-invisible men	110
to the girl who loves me only in my dreams	116
the word	117
second grade	119
today is a dynamite day from tomorrow	120
dancin dogs	122
behind the downward eye	123
if I didn't have holes in all my pockets	125
what they did in the fall	128
conquered	129
we all came weeping	131
the her	136
chemical blood	138
willow trees	143
chimes	143
darleen	145
dominoes	150
she asked me to write something	151
dinosaurs and stuff	153
the fixer	160
sock monkey in my windowsill	161
the end	162
new lacquer on an old hope chest	166

There was, there was not, a lord: and he had three sons.

And they said to their father, "We will go somewhere and begin to live."

They believed, they believed not in love.

Until they all saw a certain woman.

A princess.

And they plucked each other's eyes over who would be the one to love her.

And the youngest became the blindest and put the grass and the trees in his eyes.

And his hands became tree trunks.

And he began to see and to love.

And the princess loved him.

For in his feet were deep roots and his heart a King.

"The Three Brothers", A Bukovina Gypsy myth

I'd rather nobody saw me naked

ALL THESE HANDS ARE TREE TRUNKS

you cannot eat poems

You are not going to like this.

This isn't going to cook up in old frying pans
inside of bamboo huts with ten hungry eyes looking on.
This isn't going to be just one more day
or just one more mouthful.

This poem will not even save
one
of the 25,000 people who will starve to death today.

This is not food.

This isn't going to take to the streets
break fire-hose brigades with hunger strikes
it won't separate the pacifists from the humanists
the people from the politics.

Garrett Sherwood

This isn't going to scrape the dry blood
off of clay classroom walls
where skeletons
are still gripping onto one another's last
shhhh it's going to be alright.

This isn't going to hold babies
just a shade of love's difference
between God's greatest miracles
and quickly forgotten ghosts.

This poem will not learn to speak Setswana or Somali
or Haitian Creole
just enough to say
child, you don't have to cry today.

This is not will.

It does not replace the machete
or the machine gun
it does not replace

the needle prick or the plunger.

ALL THESE HANDS ARE TREE TRUNKS

It will not dance Irish in your heels
or Columbian in your hips
it will not taste Egyptian in your throat
or Indian on your lips.

This is not feel.
It does not punch like a kiss
or burn holes like a touch.

This will only break to bits the silence
the same way my heart's been twisted all up inside of it.

This is not love.

These three minutes and ten seconds

will not bring your neck
within breathing distance
or your chest within beating distance
or your veins within bleeding distance.

This is not apologies or
forgiveness
or gut-punchy romance.

This isn't going to pull at your bottom lip
or tease at the hem of your dress
just above your knee

Garrett Sherwood

this isn't going to take you
to the lake shore
love your ankles
and your collarbones.

This isn't going to build our bodies
into the shrine we've been praying for
this isn't going to be pictures
above the fireplace
or the steam coming from the floor.
This is not joy.
This is not strength.

This is not me.

You cannot kiss this poem
you cannot make these words feel
you
you gypsied fingers above my mind
you

this poem will not save anybody.
Not even me

And if I were not such a coward
(all the things I could do with my hands)
I don't know if I'd ever bother writing another word.

pamplona

Dust is mostly dead skin they say
but I don't think about it too much
cause then I wonder
what people are in my mouth.

I am beginning to see why people drink so much.

Call yourself a puffer fish
and maybe people won't pick so hard
at the crusty forget-me-nots
along your back.
If you're already full of air
of dust
of dead people and dead lovers

if no one wants to put a hole through you
because they're waiting for someone else to.

I am beginning to see why so many people
become bull fighters.

then you'd drown

the neighbor has so many damn bird feeders.
it's always a party.
and it makes me feel lonely.
and pecking mad.

I was going to say something
but I noticed a fatass black bird
on the satellite dish.
I told him he should get the package
with all the slutty channels.

I saw the neighbor's kids
playin on a hammock.
I asked them how come nobody ever invented
a hammock that was a hundred feet wide.
the little one said
cause then you'd drown.
the big one said
only if no one's there to save you
stupid.

ALL THESE HANDS ARE TREE TRUNKS

I said

you know how you can see shapes in the clouds?

like dinosaurs and sailboats and whatnot?

how come all I ever see

is an old man with his pants down?

they both looked up.

the little one said

oh yeah I see him

and look there's a jet stream

through his heart.

it's like I said

it's the cadillac
of skin touches
fingers to hip bones

but there's somethin to say
for the way and the angle
my body bends
the midnight dream jive
without so much
as a sly beat
to pull from the back side
of wherever it is
them fingers are

godsent

punchin cadillac fingers
that god sent

ALL THESE HANDS ARE TREE TRUNKS

they tell me the earth is tilted

I finally found the river and the sun
on the banks of the bendy wood.
Gravel road turns to glassy ripples.
There is a child nearby.
I can't see him, but I hear him.
He's learning to fish.
Something I've never done.

I'm wounding the cattlebeast.
I'm collecting the dust.
I'm eating from the copper quarry.
I'm melting down lockets.
I'm crossing off bills to pay.
I'm eating from the copper quarry.
I'm collecting the dust.

The child catches a fish.
His first one.
I can tell because I can hear him.
I hear him on the glass ripples.
Beside the bendy wood.
Where I finally found the river and the sun.

badlands and cornfields

I knew you back when we were elephants
galumphing in the badlands
puddle jumping in the bone dust
up and down the dakotas
in raincoats made of endless coastlines
big and gray and dry like our elephant bellies

back when we took the words *stomping grounds*
and embedded them in the burrow
of our makeshift bed
between Teddy Roosevelt's belt buckle
and the back seat stars
we named after Bruce Springsteen songs

I knew you back in the land where nothing grows
but the lightning
it does headstands up there
grouchy mountain cartwheels

it's where bad men go to get holy

ALL THESE HANDS ARE TREE TRUNKS

we didn't know that then
but when you were done swimming in lake hellifiknow
and you said it felt
good

repentance good

and we both agreed
we didn't deserve to stay

I knew you back when we were storm bugs
in the big corn Mecca getchyousum
glowing rhythms on a beardman's beard
while he two-fisted redpepper kernalrods
and said that his hands
were the center of the universe
since the moment he welcomed you in

back when a woman with a heavy polish accent
asked you what you would do
if you ever stopped playing ping pong
with the dreams about the last girl you loved
and the dreams about the next girl you'll lose

your answer was something about vaseline machine guns
and songs that make you think about sex

Garrett Sherwood

I knew you back in the land of thunderclouds
that looked like dirty water mop buckets
and insects that shot light out of their asses
you wondered how evolution could explain something like that
but we agreed it didn't matter
because God was in the stillness

and all you wanted to do was sit and watch the rain

I knew you back in the days of chandelier sunrises
when there was a swinging inside your chest
and an apology always on your lips
for what you thought might be too much cracking

I knew you back when we'd drive north
to get holy
and drive east
when our backs stopped bleeding
and then west again
to get the taste of resurrection
our of our mouths

back when riverbanks meant magic
and the mississippi was our grand finale

back when all we had was the road
because we couldnt get our fingertips

ALL THESE HANDS ARE TREE TRUNKS

off the steeringwheel
without everything looking brokeass
and slowmotioned
back when we couldnt get the nozzle
out of the gas tank without
feeling like we were huge
like we were pantsdropping and lipsmacking and gutsy
like our words had firebreathing crotches

I knew you back before things got slower
when the music was louder and the backbeat lower
back before the thundergrip gave way
before the granite panel wallpaper
peeled off for something less raincoat
before you noticed
what made the earth look so old
was its wrinkles
the kind you get from smiling too much

before you decided to be still

I knew you on that last day
the day you took our elephant sized saddle bags
and said you'd hold on to them for the both of us
just in case the bad came back

Garrett Sherwood

but we agreed that
profound
never looked good on you

and we left it at that

ALL THESE HANDS ARE TREE TRUNKS

this is what I think of sailboatin

like

ten thousand cupcakes

in the trunk of a convertible

goin real birdflippin fast

glovebox full of sex

stereo full of puppies

laughin and givin you money

Garrett Sherwood

big bopper

I had a dream last night that
I was the big bopper
but with a lot more faces
and with hands that stretched
from self righteousness all the way
to damn dirty shame.
I wore custom clothes.
Bandit clothes.
Made for breaking and entering.
Especially breaking.
I was looking for a name.
One for myself.
One that would make me feel something
besides skin.
Besides sin.
I crossed paths with steamboats
and airplane crash sites
looking for anybody that
could tell me that dying was alright.
That pain was for living.

ALL THESE HANDS ARE TREE TRUNKS

That someone like me,
twofaced and butchershopped,
didn't have to be breaking
and entering
all the time.

honestly

She wrestled the truth away
one finger at a time.
She asked me where the wound was
and I said
it's below my belly button
and above my brainstem.

I am a man after all.
And we come with self-destruct buttons.

leopold

He broke bullets with perverted jokes but always said sorry afterwards. He was always sorry. He would sit in the bathtub if he wasn't in his sitting chair, half filled caused he didn't want to be wasteful, watch his stomach jump to his heartbeat and think about how sorry he was and sorry and sorry and sorry and then finally got out when his dick got cold and he was sorry about that too.

He kept two journals. One for everything nice anyone ever said about him and one for every good idea he ever had. He kept them far apart, one buried in a box of old baseball trophies, the kind you get just for participating, and the other on the nightstand cause he liked the way it looked bathed in the barf light that snuck in from the street lamp through the slit between the window curtain and the wall. He looked at it sometimes in bed and tried to think of ways to save the world but instead mostly just went to sleep. He usually dreamt of flying or falling and woke up wishing he had dreamt of breasts.

He was glad he lived alone.

When he left his apartment it was mostly because he liked to ride the train. He supposed it was his best chance at someone recognizing him although it rarely happened. Just enough to fall for it.

Hey don't I know you.

Then he'd tell a perverted joke about siamese twin sheep, followed by an *I'm sorry*, and then go back to pretending to think about important things. If someone would have asked what he was thinking about he would have said, *I'm thinking of ways to do what's already been done but in a way that's far better and deeper and more thought provoking.* Then they would have said, *you're so talented,* and he'd go back to thinking about barf light on his empty notebook and breasts.

No one ever asked what he was thinking about.

On the day he saw her, the woman wearing the pink wristband and the scarf on her head that made her look like a peacock, he was wearing a dark coat and tie that reminded him of marriage. It was something he thought about a lot. He imagined her, the woman wearing the pink wristband and the scarf on her head that made her look like a peacock, in a white dress, although that didn't seem to fit. He preferred the scarf.

He thought about her with that scarf and wristband sitting in his sitting chair in his apartment. Maybe reading. Maybe reading about natural disasters. Something with vivid photography. He thought about her being

ALL THESE HANDS ARE TREE TRUNKS

there as he walked in the door. He thought about her looking at him and smiling as if to say *Welcome Home* and then looking down again at the natural disasters. He thought about her in the bath with the water almost overflowing. He thought about her laughing when he tried to make her laugh. He thought about her crying, just a little bit, every time she dreamed of hospitals, which would be often. He thought about her sleeping, with the scarf on because she never let her guard down. He thought about telling her his great ideas about saving the world every night. She would tell him that his ideas were good, but not great. He did not think about her breasts.

When he got home that day he didn't sit in his sitting chair. He didn't take a bath, half full. He didn't even think of a perverted joke to lighten the mood. And he wasn't sorry about it. Instead he went digging for his notebook buried in the baseball trophies. His sleeve got caught on the corner of a black and gold plaque that indicated something to the effect of: *you are good enough.*

He thought about her pink wristband.

He took out the notebook, ripped out the blank first page. He went to the other notebook on the barf pedestal. With a black pen he wrote on the scrap, using the notebook for a slab, something to the effect of, *hey you're that one guy.*

He thought about hospitals.

Garrett Sherwood

He folded the scrap and stuck it in the back cover of the barf book.

He looked down at his dark coat and tie. It reminded him of funerals. It was something he thought about a lot.

That night he slept in his funeral clothes staring at the notebook. He didn't care what he would dream about. He was very sorry about that.

He was glad he lived alone.

ALL THESE HANDS ARE TREE TRUNKS

1967 RV (green)(with the windows down)

sex love sans property tax

baby you had me at wheels

Garrett Sherwood

the next time I kiss you

We're gonna make mountains today.
Paint them into turtles.
Find a dog.
Call it a damn dog.
Damn dirty dog.

We're gonna make a mountain today.
Tie strings to fingers on barb wire.
She used to kiss my fingers.
I bought her lips.
She doesn't remember how I taste.
I left her at the bottom of the bottle.

I want to bite your tongue.
I want to taste your two-face tricks.
Drink my blood.
Tell me how loyal I am.
Lick the ink from my love letters.
Tell me about december.

ALL THESE HANDS ARE TREE TRUNKS

soft directions

take a handful of soaking wet momma's comin home at sunset
blackwashin the blueline clothes in the copper river

take a 6 marshmallow cheek spit
let it catch on fire
engine red
and spit it out
when it starts to smoke

take the parking lot road
to the theater
where the spring seats
make enemas out of operas

take a wordplay by the parasol
and Paris by the sun
tape them both tight to your waistband
or to your drawstring
or if you're a lady
to your bra strap

Garrett Sherwood

take a flower you've never seen
and call it a word you've never heard
and smell it in a way that makes a stranger stare

take a spoon
and then another spoon
preferably ones that go ting ting
and then play them spoons there upon your knee
that's it
just play

ALL THESE HANDS ARE TREE TRUNKS

three

nobody wanted to be the first to say
that
from the sea
their father looked more and more
like a big old oak tree

corruptible

if you were looking down on me right now

I'd be so stretched out from all the things
I have to hide

my legs in bubble gum stretch swivels
around my butterfly body

my hands on the corners of this room
my elbows crooked around my bed posts

my floor space become an art studio
I would break it to pieces

my pillow where my ear folds itself
hear my heart
I would break it to pieces

ALL THESE HANDS ARE TREE TRUNKS

my body
my body
my body

an art studio

be careful how you say those words
I'd rather nobody saw me naked

she found me in her kitchen cupboard

ALL THESE HANDS ARE TREE TRUNKS

a lesson is cosmic love connections

friday night I fell asleep listening to
Let's Get it On
on repeat

this is not a metaphor

jolly baba

As the tree grows
animate the green man.
the book of knowledge was returned to the library today
it was conveniently highlighted
gives thanks.
feels most freshly decorated
freeing up for free rainbow hugsss.
O brother, how far out thou?
see feel taste touch smell
makes sense to me
says he...

Group hug tonight??
one and all one and all.
rainbow nation of the human tribe
glueniversing along the glueniverse
glowing good glowing easy.
It's easy to see you should love one abrother
easy enough breezy
easy to me
says he....

ALL THESE HANDS ARE TREE TRUNKS

Compliments crystallize
communication clearer
rearer than clearer communication vibes.
hugging up all the cornhuggers
all inside
the center of the universe. LIVE.
sandpainting: Art of fleeting moments.
Realize
life food
a wild and coyote style.
expressive life, don't you see the wheeze?
says he...

Healersz heal on innergreat love souldate now
your choice in joy.
with the children we win.
see the spin
buttons on it, on it, on it
FOOD THE WORLD
In IN we TRUST...
WILL DANCE FOR RAIN
Dig yourself DIG THIS.
Cause it is all about the GOD particle
see the spin? happy tidbit of phraseology
says he....

Garrett Sherwood

I had a chance so I asked the world to dance
'n the light
chime of the tings
'n the middle of the sweet streets
built entirely for the Wandering Kind.
smoldering hot fresh glowing glitter daily
happiness is a good dance party
I own my bliss
I only have to put it in my feet
says he...

Genius is as Genius gets paid
part of the edgy fragilic Adult Matrix.
built up a tower unto himself
a giddy-up of gallantries and the church of rock and roll
excitlapedia of: Be the Happening!
Love is a sound, a music to my cheers
learning and rerespecting all the common decencies
says he...

Will vigor for love vibrating life
vision of camelot peaceful cities
the concert is now.
it's good for the town if you got clowns
on both sides of the kingdom
butterflies in the land of stampeding steers.
Thank GOD there are people out there like us

ALL THESE HANDS ARE TREE TRUNKS

PEACE is Aggressive
trust and ye shall be
says he...

An ah'natural neon navigation
full spectrum rainbow decision making.
so how you gonna sneeze ya way out of this
with all this BLESS YOU going on?
THE HAPPIES ARE RUNNING THIS GLOW.
Polish the inner prize. Let's fly this thing.
the center of the universe is alive and swell
see the wheeze?
says he....

for keeps

Something important just happened
and I want to be sure I don't forget it.

But just as my journal entry today
began by referring to you as her
only by the end
painting every pronoun
in second person funeral pyres
with your name printed heavy on my lips

every line becoming a letter to you
yes you

I should tell you,
I'm hoping you don't forget it either.

You sat in my corner
and I'm pretty sure you knew it was mine
it was draped in red plaid
broken zippered sleeping bags
and stacks of books by dead poets
propping up my pillow.

ALL THESE HANDS ARE TREE TRUNKS

You should know
it was not my plan to pull you so close to me.
It was not my plan to touch your hand
that way
as if there were heartsecrets embedded in your palm lines
as if there was some giant sized prize
for knowing what your fingers felt like
as if all the days I'd lived and died
had been numbered and all of them
counting down to this.

My heart rolled up
into both my hands.
The space where my heart used to be
in my chest
began to swell with hot wet regret
for each breath I'd ever spent
not begging you to come closer.

So I put one arm around you
and then the other.
I pulled you closer.

I felt you pulse.

Keep up with this.

Garrett Sherwood

It was just a boneshake of hesitation
a shiver and a single inhalation alone
of hoping for something biggersaint special.

I was hoping you'd feel it.

I was hoping that you'd feel
like you were pulling brand new strands of spine
from your back
but that there would never be sufficient back bone
to ever feel brave enough for when I finally let you go.

I was hoping that you'd feel
like a raingutter
swallowing water spouts from the sky whole
letting the raindrops rinse the dust
from your too often closed eyelids
washing twigs down your arms
across your wrists
and forever off your naked finger tips.

I was hoping you'd feel
like carving canyons from the carpet
through my breastplate
like drawing ghosts from the bottom of my chest
with each breath

ALL THESE HANDS ARE TREE TRUNKS

not thinking you could ever get enough of it
like the Morse code in your wrists
would be blaring big fast SOS
too many times to even call it
again and again.

I was hoping you'd feel
like making hand-painted ceramic plates
stacks and stacks and stacks of 'em
each one made with a different stick figure representation
of a daydreamt moment
in which I made you feel light.

I was hoping that you'd feel light.

That way, when I touched your hand for the very first time
there on that pillow of dead poets
we could both say at precisely the same moment

yeah, that's the stuff.

But instead I just mumbled quietly to myself.
Something about destiny and bad timing.

I'm not sure if you heard me.

Garrett Sherwood

But I knew
I knew from the instant
your pulse wasn't so electric
between my funeral pyre arms
it wasn't me
who should be asking you to
keep up with this.

You should know
that in an effort to be fully accountable
for all things that I am
not

I decided right then

I won't be touching you again.
I won't be pulling you in so close.
I won't be fishing for my backbone.
or burning holes through my breastplate
for you again.

Just
don't you go and forget
what my corner looks like.

It's red and plaid
and hot all over.

dancing

take my left hand.
make sure it is my left.
for in my right I hold the key
to the biggest abandoned ballroom in town.
under my arm are the shiniest
black dancing shoes.
around my neck is the most
perfectly proportioned bow tie.
on my head is the smoothest
groomed head of hair.
in my front pocket is most
brightly colored handkerchief.
my pants are the type that glide.
my cuffs are properly linked.
my socks are the fancy kind.
and slung over my shoulder
is a rainbow colored hammock
the size of just you and me
to hang up in the abandoned ballroom
to swing just above the floor

and forget all that dancing nonsense.

Garrett Sherwood

the little girl

you were the first girl I ever saw naked.
we were six years old.
spent the whole day catchin crawdads.
soaked and wiggly cold.
they took our clothes off.
wrapped us in big green towels.
yours slipped for a second.
I was confused.
and in love.

the day she moved away

she took a hundred hearts
in her mom jeans pockets.
her bones had piano strings in them.
on the playground she danced.
only the black keys.
before the bell brought the boys
down from the jungle gyms.
magic-pantsed and jaw-boned.
where they'd been watching her
and singing along softly.

this right is not always

sweet

tell me where those knuckles have been

unclench them for me

write me letters that end in exclamation points

show me how to catch rain

open mouthed and hands reaching

chase me under the stadium bleachers

let me take you to the highest rooftop in this town

tell me why you have a favorite star

I'll tell you why I call every mountain mine

get your fingers up underneath my wrists

ALL THESE HANDS ARE TREE TRUNKS

show me pictures of old russian women

the ones with handprints deep in their wrinkles

I'll say it makes me feel like God

help me remember my dream last night

tell me it means we're dying

tell me the last time you cried for no reason

draw me pictures of your favorite color

drink water like it was made of diamonds

break fasts like a lumberjack

steal your hips from the hanged crescent moon

read my stories off of my neck veins

I'll write my poems along your backbone

I'll write my name along your backbone

Garrett Sherwood

drive with me to mexico

hit the gas the moment we see we're starting to fall

tell me you would love me forever

if only you knew how

I'll say samesies

call me a liar

but don't you mean it

ALL THESE HANDS ARE TREE TRUNKS

the girl who always sat by the window and the boy who always say behind her

he loved her like the emergency door of an airplane

silently
and full of courage

the bug catcher

1. She
entered me not through the top
or the hip
but around and around and around
so many times around
I did not see through her
until that night my toes were frozen
to my brake pedal in Bend, Oregon
sleeping off six months

that night I dreamt of
collapsible bird cages

that night I dreamt of
scraping paint-on wood grain off
of photosinister pulpits
where people dressed as mailmen
gave my body away
for 37 cent stamps and a pack of
cigarettes hard and fuzzy
special price cause I already
dug my bones

ALL THESE HANDS ARE TREE TRUNKS

half way to her
when she went lookin.

2. She found
inside of me
flower-pot shape heart-picks
along the back walls
behind the racing striped camera boxes
pointing crisscrossed towards
the cardboard corneas in the front
with a heavy ply of floor board
rattle snares across the two
lines of sight intentionally
laid bare except for the
red encrusted curtains that were
only visible in the sun
hanging parallel but passive
against the wolf trap stencils
to the right
and the burlap bag
full of starter pistols
to the left

that was all it took.

3. She found me
in her kitchen cupboard
straddling the vinegar
and the spice rack

she told me she loved me
as I drove away the next day
but we both knew that
you love the butterfly
not the bug catcher

she buried my bones
for a 37 cent stamp
and a Polaroid

she said it was of me
but I saw from a distance
that it was a tree
lightninbolt split in half

that night I dreamt
of tilting banana trees
and broken brake lights

that night I dreamt
of holy cork-board finger paintings
and hands I just couldn't get clean.

bathtub poems

I wish we had a painting of a freight train
but that would be too sexy.

If I was better with puns I would say
Let's do Chicago like Howlin Wolf.

I wonder if you'd like me even more
if I was made of ice cream cones.
You'd probably slobber all over me.
But I'd be okay with that.

Every night right after you fall asleep
I tell you a new secret.
They're all about wanting to sex you up.

You laugh like a box of old polaroids.
I'm a fiend for this.
That's why I dream of flashing bulbs
and trigger sweat.

Your skin reminds me of ribbons on christmas presents
like skimming the top of wheat fields with open hands.

Garrett Sherwood

Except I don't want to gnaw on wheat fields.

And baby you're crunchy.

Do you remember when we were just couch lovin
and asked me about forever?

Well I would tell you but these bubbles are underwhelming
and I don't want to give away the ending just yet.

ALL THESE HANDS ARE TREE TRUNKS

I write about these people

as if there is nothing better to do than get caught fishin in the wishin well

Garrett Sherwood

big empty house

Playing loud music in a big empty house
full of big empty memories
'sgot my soul on fire.
I'm heading north tomorrow.
I'm heading north tomorrow.

There are two trees: one perfect and tall
the other twisted and turned just like me.
I can't climb them both but even if I could
I don't think I would
for the ground is not nearly as giving as the God
who twisted me up unforgiven in the first place
placing tightly wound seeds
underneath my fingertips and in my toes
expecting me to grow and to stay golden unrusted.
But truth is it doesn't matter
what tree I climb
because truth is my fruit is only sweet until the second bite
and truth is I dont even really know why
but there must be a reason
something worth believing.
So I used the foreclosed sign

ALL THESE HANDS ARE TREE TRUNKS

to break the back window
of that Big Empty House,
the place where God made me.

Memories, mostly hollow
bounce whispers off these once meaningful walls.
I put my ear up to them hoping to hear
something.
Some moan or a groan
It wouldn't have mattered
if it was something
but there was nothing
so I cut my hands open and collapsed them down
in semicircles
smoothing out the lumps
till all my prints are equally inked.
And I press them to the white white walls
to see if the wet red match
the old black marker traced ones
that I thought I should've recognized
and they did.

So I reached deep into my abdomen,
grabbed my sopping wet stomach
and began to twist the memories out of it.

Garrett Sherwood

Did you know there used to be carpet here?
I swear, it's crawled off somewhere
but there used to be carpet here.
Carpet where my father's arms slammed me down.
Carpet where my mother's tongue cut my soul
into so many pieces I could not count them.
Carpet that burned against my skin.
But I'm not burning against the sins of my parents
no
because at least that was something.
At least blood boiled in my father's arms.
At least the picture my mother's tongue
painted was crimson and violet.
And at least my tears were salty and real.
But these walls
this house
this college of infectious introversion
sold to myself in a guise of introspection.
This museum of man who's still just a boy
who spends all his lonesome hours
scribbling in notebooks and making doodles of flowers.
A boy who instead of playing with other kids
grabbed books and a guitar
and locked himself in a basement.
A boy
who never could tell the girl he loved her
because he didn't know how

ALL THESE HANDS ARE TREE TRUNKS

and he still doesn't.

But this house
did not make me.
It was God who made me
and He made me twisted
but he also made me perfect
and there is perfectly twisted poetry in this heart
just like the chandelier that's seldom lit
a crown without a king
Poetry.
There are rivets across my chest and back
holding up all my loose ends and fractured skin
shred to indecence
from each time I went searching for something more.
Rivets
that if you look just right,
paint grand pictures of rivers and oceans.
Rivets
that if you put a record player needle
against my skin
it would play soaring arias
sung by beautiful women.

So I get an electric guitar
and I drag it through
that busted back window

and I get the biggest speaker I can find
and turn all the little knobs all the way to the right
and wearing nothing but a broken foreclosed sign
rub my bloody hands
up and down the six silver beauties
till angels and devils come pouring out of me

and I shake the doors and rattle the windows
and bounce the floors like a heart in my hand
and I crack that chandelier in half
and a million tiny fireflies
find their way into my fingers
and into my toes

and there
there
I made God
created in my own image.
A king without a crown.
A boy with no friends and no answers.
A man who only speaks of burning
so much burning.

So I'm heading north tomorrow
this big empty house
'sgot my soul on fire.

ALL THESE HANDS ARE TREE TRUNKS

on our way to Portland

I promised you a love letter.
I smashed a headlight instead.
An omen of my body.
A dead deer.
We named him Lloyd.
I'm pretty sure it was a girl deer.
I made promises to your outline.
You filled me in red.
I never let you go.
You put me in your chest.

Garrett Sherwood

I've come to kill you all. big fisted.

ALL THESE HANDS ARE TREE TRUNKS

baldassare

1.

I cut my hand on the hardpan today.
It was the first time I said your name since you left.

I had always thought that if you loved me
as much as I loved this pick axe
if you would have built me up
with as much bramble and sawdust
as I pulled gutted from the ground
if you would have brought me water
to rinse the dynamite smoke from my skin

we could've hid here always.

I don't actually remember when you left
months
or years

I was digging forever before you
I am digging forever since.

Garrett Sherwood

2.
I used to sleep on my back
and dream of fishes swimming like stars
just a breath
beyond my arm's reach away

and now
I sleep on my stomach
and forget that they're still there
swimming
like stars.

I don't suppose you remember this

all you remember is the digging.

I've discovered that the nights
I've not well slept with my ribs feeling bonesplit
up to my eyelids
have become the ones
I most prefer

because I don't care to dream any more
when all my dreams
are digging dreams.

ALL THESE HANDS ARE TREE TRUNKS

3.

Funny how mostly when I think of you
I think
of the things you called my hands

cameltongued dirtsplintered rosethorned
nitroglistened axepickgnarled backbonemongered
rockspitinfested machinebirthed bloodbickered
cowhiderotten morningfogcrossed
obsessive earthy emancipated hands.

There was that day a bird stumbled
petrified and heavenreaching
down the steps
to the hole I dug for you
for us.

I was about to reach out to it
but you forbade me

your hands
you said
your hands.

idaho

she pulled at his slumber beach bottom lip
with her motel teeth
and put her Karl Marx hands in his
coat pockets

Idaho is cold in the winter
but she didn't want to remember it that way

she was heading for New Orleans
like a box of lightbulbs and firecrackers
and he held her just as carefully
but only till she stopped burning

he pulled away slip fingered and rock face palmed
till the string snapped around her
record player eyes
broken with
this is goodbye
skip
this is goodbye
skip
this is goodbye

ALL THESE HANDS ARE TREE TRUNKS

in this book

Am I a man who pours lonely from cereal boxes?

I ain't no prize darlin

I'd rather crunch your hips between my teeth
and still leave room between my cheeks
for what you'd call dancers' sweat

nineteen-fifty-eight is the only time lately
that seems to know what I'm sayin

because them boys back then

they knew how to dream

without wrists and fingertips
but with stream sing-songs and matching outfits

they made their women sound like wine-glasses

they beat their guitars and their guitars beat back

Garrett Sherwood

my love

I could not give you up for Portland

or for black and white movies

or for books about the sun

but I ain't no nineteen-fifty-eight

and you ain't no punchline darlin

the middle

we tucked our feet up inside ourselves
hoping to stay warm.

we said
1 2 3   shoot.
you pulled rock.
and I pulled stitches.
we both went away losers
after we agreed
that you were too good for me.
and I never learned to be happy.

you told me I wouldve made an interesting sculpture
the way I kept my head down
when I let you leave.

Garrett Sherwood

while the faucet is running

how long till you get your feet wet
depends on which way youre heading
he told me

he told me it was the land of that
ten thousand reasons
to be afraid of motor boats comin too close
and choppin your damn head off
ten thousand reasons
why starin out the window
in the breakroom of the 40th floor office
makes you see targets on everybody's back

the land of 10,000 hours
until you master something
like how to smile
when they got you by your neck skin

he told me about dreams
dreams with jackhammers stuck in them
shakeful
dreams of mold and burnt eyebrow stink

ALL THESE HANDS ARE TREE TRUNKS

he asked me what happens
when your old dreams
and new dreams
are playing a shootout game
across the rocky mountains

and what happens when the God
you've been praying to
gives you everything you ask for

but it sucks

he says it's hard to pray anymore
and it was easier when he wasnt so sure
that God loved him

he says maybe he'll find a new God
one that doesn't like to be bothered

he says now that's trust

looking out the 40th floor window
he says
when the flood comes
he wants to be the first
to taste the bathwater

why tiresmashed squirrels are not squirrels but something else entirely

1.

Standing in front of a sign that read
Thrift Store is Down the Stairs
a woman called out to me
and said
Where is the Thrift Store?

I said
It's down the stairs.

I wondered if she was an idiot.

2.

My road has black spots that used to be red spots.
No one ever says
poor damn black spots.

3.

Later that same day
someone probably asked that woman
a stupid question.

ALL THESE HANDS ARE TREE TRUNKS

4.

When you smash something

it makes you feel really really friggin big.

5.

And she probably wondered

if they were an idiot.

Garrett Sherwood

the things I would tell him

I. the stagecoach

there was one day I remember
when the ghosts didn't bother me so very much
and I was nice to everybody
and everybody was nice to me

I wish my father had met me on that day

most mornings there are invisible people
holding love thickwristed over me
laying blows into the ribcage storage
where everything that has been made desert
is put away

these are usually the type of days
in which my father meets me

he combs back my head long hair
he picks two nice things
to say about my face
and one thing I could work on

ALL THESE HANDS ARE TREE TRUNKS

about my back
how to keep it as close to being straight
as I can

he spares me from absolutes
always at first
I wonder what he thinks he's saving me from

but today is not one of those days
today I've armed myself to meet him
I have a stagecoach
full of letters I've written to him
it's been readied by the light of the colt revolver

I'm riding shotgun
not driving
this is because I know my father is the type
that appreciates the unheralded one

besides
he always dreams in terms of cowboys

II. the letters

the letters would be all the justincase things
that I would tell him
such as

dear dad
just in case the hollows of my fortune cookies
break open fortuneless from here on out

dear dad
just in case all these smart phones get way too smart
and we get way too lazy to talk anymore

dear dad
just in case
I was right about what makes good people good
and bad people bad

just in case
I was wrong

just in case
the rapture happens and we end up on different sides
of the great white lie

ALL THESE HANDS ARE TREE TRUNKS

just in case
you weren't the man I thought you were

just in case
you're more a man than I'll ever be

just in case
you'll one day be proud of me

just in case
I one day have a son who reminds me of you

just in case
my beard grows so big
you won't be able to think of me as a boy anymore

just in case
you find out I've secretly been voting democrat
all these years

just in case
you find out
okay
I don't actually vote at all

just in case
you weren't able to pull me

Garrett Sherwood

from the river in time

just in case
the music takes me

just in case
it was that headfirst fall when I was three years old
that made me who I am

just in case
I never see you again

just in case
your surgery doesn't go so well

just in case
you're gone before I get home for Christmas

just in case
it's all over
all of it

every word
even love

just in case
there's no such thing

ALL THESE HANDS ARE TREE TRUNKS

just in case
you were too busy paying bills and buying presents
to be my father

just in case
I was too busy chasing dreams and fighting ghosts
to be your son

just in case
I find the right words
the perfect words
in the perfect moment for speaking words
when both our theme songs
are pouring out in buckets
just like in the movies
but we still say nothing

Garrett Sherwood

III. the things

the things I would tell that man

these things
they fill me up
fill me up to my hands
up my almost straight back
but they never reach my mouth

I suppose I get that from him

ALL THESE HANDS ARE TREE TRUNKS

when the cynic gets happy he drive faster

writing was always easier when I had
more hell in my bones

it's like looking for a party to crash
one you know all your ex-girlfriends will be at

like imalivin film strip
of car crashes

bloody asphalt

strange how it doesn't make you think
that maybe you should slow down

just that everybody else should

Garrett Sherwood

I saw a ghost today

I shoulda let you screw me
that way we'd both be broken

ALL THESE HANDS ARE TREE TRUNKS

church of chainsaw silence

inside my mouth there is just more skin
and honkey tonk girls.
there is dancing.
the days are numbered in there.
but they are in roman numerals
and after about a hundred and four
nobody cares anymore
cause if it looks like a sieve
and if we're gonna be sinking
then we might as well be dancing.
heartstitched and overplayed.
tonguetied and kneeshake.
hipshot.
boneshot.

my tongue is a slipslide summer.
drinking from the hose.
back when nothing ever tasted so good.
not even the marbles in your pocket.
when every girl looked so shiny
in their one piece bathing suits.
shiny and tall.

Garrett Sherwood

in my teeth streets
there are apocryphal pocket sized dictionaries
filled with all the sounds we make
between the words
but above their meanings.
I pick them from my back molars
with my slipslide tongue.
broken glass.
manifest stuttery.
there is
ooing and ummin and errring.
libraries of it.
on both sides of the teeth street.

in the gutter there is a church
with a child inside.
he doesn't have knees
so he bows with his mouth.
he doesn't believe in forgiveness
so he just prays for bigger hands.
he wants to hold more in.
there is ink on his fingertips.
there is ink on his lips.
black.
he wants to hold it in.

ALL THESE HANDS ARE TREE TRUNKS

outside the church
there are chainsaws.
a whole parade of chainsaws.
they look like a dragon.
it's dancing.
the honky tonk girls are ooing.
the tall shiny girls are slipping through his legs.
they are slipping through my teeth
the boy stays inside with his hands over his mouth.
I got him between my molars.
I say
crunch man crunch.
he doesn't make a sound.

in the gutter there is a church.
it belongs to heaven
but it was built by my father.
there are butterflies in the boney rafters.
every once in awhile they beat in time
to the swing of saloon doors.
people come for miles.
they say
there
they can see God dancing.
and drinking from the hose.

chloe

One
I'm painting over the spot
Chloe is cool
knuckle etched bonefist bare
on the windowsill overlooking the garbage cans
by Chloe. etchfist.
I'm filling the lines
two second swipes
whiteblood jailcells
where dear Chloe took the time
toe nail file
purple finger fight
to make a permanent note to herself
that she is
cool

Two
Chloe
when you dug the devil out of this
windowsill
I hope you meant it forever
I hope you dreamt of a world without banks

ALL THESE HANDS ARE TREE TRUNKS

where every home was a home forever
and every scuff and scrit
was a pledge to your children's children
that they too could be etched into
the cool category
and I hope you filled your claws
with as much paint and drywall
as they could carry
when they dragged you outta here

in the dark

there was that night we reminisced
on our various first kisses
under that blanket of whispers
that buckled our mouths
but split open our souls

and you asked
if I thought we'd ever have another

and I said
not on this continent

that's when you said
you wouldn't say you loved me
in case it ended up in a poem

and I said
there's too much dirt
under my fingernails anyway

ALL THESE HANDS ARE TREE TRUNKS

strawberry moon

we are all landscape dancers tonight.
valley underground heroes
and starry night bandits.
for we too cut our parachutes
from our safety nets
we squeeze the cinder
from our afterthoughts.
and we bleed.
hot and sweet.

darling you don't have to act your age
cause you weren't born to be that way
and the devil isn't to me what it is to you
because to you it might be the truth about
what your hands have been doin.

I only care about whether or not
these sprinklers turn on
to make it feel more like the movies
when we do these cartwheels
we been handclaspin God for
and whether or not

Garrett Sherwood

I make myself slap belly laugh

like you
so you know you're not the only one
with your fingers crossed
when you put your big boy shoes back on.

no
tonight we are barefeet.
tonight we stuff feathers in our pockets.
pass the moon between our fingertips.
you say breathe deep.
spaceman deep.
we kiss the sagesmoke.
you are on fire.
I have strawberry seeds in my teeth.
someone is dancing.
someone is counting dandelions in the dark.
someone climbs a tree.
someone climbs all the trees.
and the big stone wall.
I say I am a murder poet.
I've come to kill you all.
big fisted.
we all go tumbling.
and land indian style.
knees knocking.

ALL THESE HANDS ARE TREE TRUNKS

I pull at the grass.
build a body from the dandelion stems.

I say poems.
we all say all the poems.
we do cartwheels.
but the sprinklers don't turn on.
we cut our parachutes from our safety nets.
our fingertips are redstained and sweet.
someone says make a picture.
but no one brought the black paint.
we make our shadows fight.
long and skinny.
moon shadows.
kung fu shadows.
I lay down again.
I want to tell stories.
I want everyone to tell stories.
laying down and hands reaching.
you put the kombucha between my legs.
for safe keeping.
I say I'm not sleeping.
you say me neither.
someone climbs a tree.

I tell you a story.

Garrett Sherwood

when I was a child I used to catch arm-fulls of fireflies
and stuff them into plastic bottles
pretending I was God making the night
glow in my hand
and now that I'm older
I smash heart shaped gongs that sound
like glass machine guns
shooting sparkcrackle bombs
at the old jukebox love songs
that keep my throat burning
like a bottle of fireflies
and I wonder if these
truly are the good ol' days.

darling
we have the moon between our breastplates.
and strawberries between our kisses.

and I've been saying your name for decades.

and the ghosts still shouted

Garrett Sherwood

one thousand miles per hour

1.
When the human body goes from one thousand miles per hour
to zero
in the browbeat and the blinksnap
the whole damn thing explodes
starting with the heart
and then working its way out to the fingertips.

We all know how this feels

it's what happens when the earth stops spinning.

2.
I'm 26 years old and I still believe in fairytales like infinity.

I believe
because sometimes
I jump in the shower and forget how to make myself clean.

Because I get confused
what the word afterlife is supposed to mean.

ALL THESE HANDS ARE TREE TRUNKS

Because one time on a train in Chicago
with three of my friends
the smart one said that
statistically speaking
one of us might not make it
to the age I am now
and we wondered which of us
that would be.

I believe
because dreams are the only time
we're not actually spinning.

So there must me a whole bunch more out there
I still can't see.

That same night on that train
the four of us
handspit promised
that if we ever got rich we'd take care of each other.

It took me ten years to figure out what he meant
when the smart one said
that making promises while saying
only if
is probably the universe's way of telling you
that you suck.

Garrett Sherwood

I learned it with a phone call bomb.

The voice said it happened an hour ago
exactly one thousand miles east of here.
The smart one was alone.
It was his way of showing
he stopped believing in infinity
starting with his heart
working out to his fingertips
and onto the bathroom floor.
There's a perch on the universe's elevator door.
It has his name on it now.
From the time I hang up the phone
to when they put the stars around him
I spin by him twice more.
I've been keeping my hands open
hoping to hold him close
the tenyearsago him
that told the tenyearsago me
to just let it go.
Back when he said infinity
is everything that you cannot see.
Back when he still believed
in the crossstitch of the spinning dream.
Before the eye became the beam.
Before we reached for bottles

ALL THESE HANDS ARE TREE TRUNKS

like we forgot how to breathe.

Before we took our childhood
and gave it to the razorblades
to the spitsoaked highways
to the back seats of the love we craved.

Before I said I promise

only if.

I wonder if afterlife is just a word that means we owe something
for all the people we let die alone.

3.
The smart one once told me that
scientists say if the earth stopped spinning the air
would just keep on moving
at a thousand miles an hour
and cut us all right the cuss in half.

I asked him
hamburger ways or hotdog.

He said he would get back to me on that
but either way
it would probably begin at your heart.

the hunt

at nights he dreamt of
fortune cookies
and other things that told him
she'd been there before

alan and me

When I first saw him
he was walking uphill all elbows and knees
a king kong apparition
with holes punched through
his punchy black shirt
like gunshots through a parachute.
We talked about
TV screen fingerprints and finger TV screens
his tumbleweed voice
broke on me like a motorcade.
I asked him where he was goin
and he said
second story itchiness and dreams about ghosts
and we decided we oughta go there together.

Except for his arms
his body
fit through a slot in a vending machine
between my fingers
between the crack in my windshield
and except for his arms
which I named

Garrett Sherwood

arm-ageddon and mr. veiny
he slipped in my car.

We got to his place
and his boxcut knuckles
broke into snaptalic steam engines
with wolfbreath and forehead sweat
and scuttle love.
He asked me what my favorite car was
I said thunderbird
and he went and got a box
from the back
full of tiny bits of thunderbird.

I hesitated
but through his broken bottle teeth
he said
just jump on in.
The wilderness of his sitstand hands
and canadian-rules football veins on his neck
erased the earnestness of his kickstomach eyes.
And so I jumped on in.
I asked him to tell me stories while we built.

He told me about schoolyard romance
and the girl he loved like his favorite fairytale.

ALL THESE HANDS ARE TREE TRUNKS

He called her his girlfriend
cause there's no other word for it.
He told me about her father
who made F-16 sounds
when he barked.
He told me about pulpit pranksters
who burnt forktongued prophecies
into his hands because he prayed better than they did.
He told me about copshows
how they made him feel bulletproof.
He told me about his bicycle
he called it his vehicle
and said it soared the most
when he felt the loneliest.
He told me how he'd feel invisible all the time
if it weren't for his mouth tasting so bloodhot
to remind him he's alive.
He told me he liked to laugh in the snow
and blow kisses to the rain.
He told me about ghosts
and said one day he'd tell me how his arms
got so big
but not today.

He told me about his notebook
where he wrote all his stories.

He called it
stories of the undergods.
I imagined his arms like faucets turned to red
writing with steam.
He went and got a shoebox from the bathroom
he shook it like a bundle of rainsticks
against his burlap skin
and said
These are the undergods.

He popped a cap and threw an orange bottle back
like he was drinking the last bit of milk from the bowl.

The next day I gave him a ride to his girlfriend's house
but we never got there
just drove in circles
he didn't seem surprised
I guess I wasn't either.

I asked him how his arms got so big

he said
Holding on all the time.

The last time I saw him
he was still all elbows and knees
but I thought

ALL THESE HANDS ARE TREE TRUNKS

Alan

you look more Jesus than six shooter to me.

But then again
God holds this man
up
whiplashed
so what do I know.

february fifteenth club for non-invisible men

This poem predates the previous one, but they are both the same story told two different ways, at two different times in my life.

Yesterday Alan flinched
and fell straight out from heaven
on his brand new bicycle.

Silence-esque was his own form of patriotism
in a wholly black filthy teeshirt
with holes of holy white bright ambition
peeping tommed through
to his robinhood hands
raw from the glue
of a year of glue-together model cars
and fingertips
against convex TV glass.

He liked to feel the cop show re-runs.

It was a year of chaining and rechaining
his brand new bicycle to the kitchen table
dreaming of gravel.

ALL THESE HANDS ARE TREE TRUNKS

A year of opening and closing
and opening and closing
boxes.
Boxes full of bottles.
Bottles full of tiny white promises
that his only friends
the ones that spin
up and back inside his head
would be splattered like old coffee stains
on the inside of his eyelids.

He figures if God wants to preach to him
through his bedroom nightlight
well that was just fine.

But that's not what they tell him
so he takes his boxes full of bottles
and throws back those tiny white bits
of invisible lonely down.

But yesterday
Alan flinched.
The bottles shook empty.
The TV screen didn't hum so loudly.
His bicycle didn't look so tame.
His hands were bugeyed and thirsty.
And Alan let his braveheart out

Garrett Sherwood

He glanced bloodpumpingly at the hallmarked February day
and with a pink flower without a name taped to his back
a ring box without a ring
in the pocket of his only black pants

he pedaled hard and he pedaled fast.

There was a soaring falcon
of a woman out there
and she was waiting for him
diving off his memories
through the air to the door
that would let him in
to the places that would only seem like dreams
if not for all the ghosts
shouting
dear Alan
keep pedaling.

He began to make true love histories
from the heart shaped smoke rings
he huffed into the frigid february air
while ghosts still shouted
dear Alan you're almost there.

His body right-angled up to heaven
but his bones bending

ALL THESE HANDS ARE TREE TRUNKS

his nostrils reaching
for something less invisible
than that girl
the ghosts were guiding him to.

Not this door not that
not this street but the other
his circles grew
bigger, then smaller, then bigger,
and then
it began to snow.

And Alan stopped pedaling.

He felt for the flower without a name
on his back.
He felt for the ringbox without a ring
in his pocket.
And then he tried to think of her face.
Gone gone gone.

He thought
Only a crazy person
would be out here in the snow.

So alone.

Garrett Sherwood

He walked his old bicycle
all the way home
chained it to his kitchen table
and spent the rest of the darkest night
speaking in psalms to his nightlight.

He pulled his shoulder blades apart
and dragged his shaky hands
up through his tortured silver hair
begging for air
opening dryly his brick colored lips.

But the ghosts still shouted.

Dear Alan
do not close up your heart
your dreams may be invisible
but you are not
you
Alan
you
you wire of man
you hag tooth rockefeller
you opal hush poet
you minuscule Sasquatch
you are a Renaissance of odds and ends
a cracked joke of an angel

ALL THESE HANDS ARE TREE TRUNKS

no Alan
you are not invisible.

He sat tall like a feather never falling
gave thanks to his God
and the voices in the nightlight
turned on the TV
lied down in front of it
and fell hard
hard asleep.

Garrett Sherwood

to the girl who only loves me in my dreams

I still hope you come back again tonight

though it took me forty-seven minutes
to pick up the pieces this morning

forty-seven reasons why I'm no crowbar
and you're no lock pick

I still pull the pins from the door frame
and stretch a landing pad across the window sill

I'm sleeping now

come back to me

the word

The man saw cherry blossoms on the God spit spinning like roasted lamb wherever he went. The splits in the asphalt chewed through the slavelevy leather soles in his shoes but he said that this was a gift. In one hundred degree summers there are one hundred and one reasons to do anything but this and he knew it but his gospel grip of red sea split knuckles on pocket sized bibles, salvation you can carry, was embroidered in his door to door smile.

A woman opened the door enough to put her face through and the top half of half her fingers. Her fingernails were blue-green but were faded to exactly the same color as the door but the man didn't notice that. Only that they were all cracked.

What are you selling?

Miracles on every little page. Salvation you can carry.

I need miracles but not the little paper kind.

The woman closed the door but it didn't make a sound. The man thought that even the door looked sweaty. And hungry. He put his slipstitched fingers up to the door and dragged them across the part that reminded him of God. He traced the down and then the across. From top to bottom and from left to right. A piece of blue-green chipped off in his hand. He said it was a gift.

The man unviced his book hand. The leather cover was warped with gospelheat and knucklespit. He placed it on the ground leaning against the blue-green door. There were cherry blossoms saved in his pockets and he put the blue-green door chip in his pocket beside them. He thought perhaps the woman was still on the other side of the door listening to him.

God bless you.

And on and on.

ALL THESE HANDS ARE TREE TRUNKS

second grade

every single day in second grade
I watched your hands pretend to play the piano
on the divot where your pencils were supposed to go

we sat next to each other
so I had no choice
but to fall in love with you

Garrett Sherwood

today is a dynamite day from tomorrow

if all days

were made out of today

there wouldn't be enough white space
on my peach crayon skin
to tattoo all the places I've been
starting with my bed
and ending with my bedroom door

it amounts to the rising up
feet on the ground
four steps
right hand reach
open the door
and walk right through it

and I do this because I'm hungry.

I do this because of the seven billion neurons firing
from my bed to the door
at least a handful are fixing up

ALL THESE HANDS ARE TREE TRUNKS

an old banner in firecracker red letters
with the pledge I made one year ago
and the subtext
you did it

you
you did it
just you, two hands in the shape of a sledgehammer
you

today is the last day
of the days that lead me to tomorrow

and when I finally walk out that door
in seven billion moments
I ask myself

of those seven billion bursts
how many were chainsaws
and how many were hummingbirds?

and I firecrack back

all of them

dancin dogs

she wore a scarf around her head
told me mickey hart was god
but only if there is such a thing
she said soul was for people
with debts to pay
she looked at her three legged dog when she said that
but he didn't look back
just danced
I wore a blue sweater with a hole over the left shoulder
it reminded me of knife fights
the inside out kind
the kind that leaves you hummin
like a pit snake sweetie
at least that's what she said
when she covered the hole
with her hand

ALL THESE HANDS ARE TREE TRUNKS

behind the downward eye

I told her
yes, drop on by

we tussle twisted fingers
along the top of the couch
it reminds me of canopies and cradles
the way this couch is being undervalued

a band plays in the TV box

I fixed the clicker the other day
dead batteries
I took the ones from the alarm clock

but I don't tell her that

it was reminding me of how often
these last four months
I wanted to tell her I missed her

we haven't spoken in four months

Garrett Sherwood

I change the channel

she mentions how tired I look
I say
it's been a weird day

I think
at least I can sleep in tomorrow

I try to tell her with my mind
that I wish she would sit closer to me

and then she does

ALL THESE HANDS ARE TREE TRUNKS

if I didn't have holes in all my pockets

We could dance together.
The way they do in the movies.
Like hummingbirds were in our chests
and fireflies in our eyes
like we both knew something secret
from the way our hips kept gliding
back and forth
to find each other.

We could both get a big stupid smile on our face
every time we saw one of those things
memory lovestroked just for us.
Maybe not something so big bawdy
but precious still for the piece of our love story
it would open musicboxed in our brains.
Maybe it could be haystacks or six-string banjos
or apples cut sideways so you can see the star
who knows?

We could make believe
that every night was the night
before the radio was invented

Garrett Sherwood

and that the jazz spinnin off the record player
would be ours and only ours
but only for twelve more hours
and that's all the excuse we would need
to let the walls hear our bones
and the ringing of our bodies
counting down to tomorrow.

I could find out if there really is a difference
between loving someone
and dreaming about loving someone
because one of those definitely feels more real than the other
but it might not be the one you'd expect.
In my dreams there is no amount of broken bits of spine
that could keep me from forgetting
everything
everything everywhere
except the way she looked that night
when she began to sit just a little bit closer to me.

We could both make peace offerings every single day.
not for any tongue lashed back bites
but for every bit of life we let stutter wingless
in our hands
before we figured out what Etta James
been singin about all this time.

ALL THESE HANDS ARE TREE TRUNKS

Love.
At last
the big love.

I could make sketches of us
on brightly colored construction paper.
Leave you love letters
on the steamed up bathroom mirror
after every shower.
We could make pinatas from the wanted section
of sunday morning's newspaper.
Make pilgrimages to the spots
where we first stole each other's glances.
Inscribe our initials into every bed post and oak tree
we ever met.

I could make it easier.
Like the way a sunrise comes from red slices
to big burning waltz on the skyline
in the moment just before you close your eyes
so too
we could jump from young wanderlovers
with fingers in each other's hair
to gray whisperers of sweet nothings
into one another's hearing aid filled ears
all in the moment just before we close our eyes.

Garrett Sherwood

what they did in the fall

she grabbed him by his autumn leaves
piles and piles
they crackled as they fell into each other

ALL THESE HANDS ARE TREE TRUNKS

conquered

I can hear your skin and your eyes and your fingers
and the way the artificial lighting attaches to your hair

Garrett Sherwood

in the gutter there is a church

ALL THESE HANDS ARE TREE TRUNKS

we all came weeping

1. dear woman
you never once thought of yourself as beautiful
but your arms swing like butterfly doors
when you dance
and your face twists like fig trees
when your favorite song comes on
and when you breath out
there is nothing but blues
on your breath

and woman
you are beautiful

I know I came to you thrashing
and that all I left you was bleeding
but I was just a cut throat
begging for someone
to confess they made me do it
I said it might as well be you

and that's where we began
you and me

Garrett Sherwood

skin frayed
and fingers crossed
like umbilical cords

2. you took a brow beating
from my outstretched arms
the day I told you I didn't need you
anymore
I explained that you were just a shell
I came screaming out of
a blunderbuss of blood
and sexual concept
a construct of breaking hips
and lightswitch romance
I said you were just a raincloud
and a dust bowl
a fish hook
with bones stretching out to everywhere
and I couldn't see through you
anymore

I hesitated when the screen door slammed shut
hoping the crackbang would break you big wide open
hoping you'd drag your fingernails down my back
before you ever let me leave like that

ALL THESE HANDS ARE TREE TRUNKS

woman

you hit your sorries

like hammerthrows

your I forgive yous

like left hooks

your hair always reminded me

of wilting roses

you got your knuckles

flintlocked

and your feet

sparkplugged

and you were not born to be anything

but punchy

3. woman

I wanted to be lovesocked

and haymaker romanced

I wanted more

I wanted you to tell me

that I couldn't have breakfast

until I did something brilliant

I wanted you to tell me

that stars were made of magic

and so were watermelons

that the holes in my heart
only meant that I was holy
and that was the only way to feel God

that I wasn't too good for love
that you weren't too bad for it

that you didn't dream of pill bottles
just like I didn't dream of ambulances

cause woman
we got that same stripmine look in our eyes
we're built from the same scrapyard
we both got forearms like coffee cans
shoulder blades like blenders
hip bones like an airplane propeller
and a stomach full of spare change and rocks

so you need to know
that I couldnt break you
without breaking me too

4. I remember
when I used to hear sirens
and wonder which of us they were coming for

ALL THESE HANDS ARE TREE TRUNKS

when I used to belt buckle
my white knuckles
to my cassette player
to keep them from crashing against your door
again

when I used to listen
to blues compilations and count
the ways those songs made more sense to me
than you

I know I came to you weeping

and that all you remember is the thrashing

and I'm sorry I never told you
but woman
you're beautiful

the her

She said *forever*.
but it wasn't that.

It was the crossstich in her lips
and the stormcloud of begettin
bein begot in her cheeks.

I've never believed in superlatives
but there is such thing as perfection.

The first stroke of peach colored paint
on the hammernail country summer sunset
all punchy and whatnot.

See
if you believe in grape juice
and watermelon seed spittin
if you believe in red checkered picnic blankets
then you believe in fairytales.

I remember the feel of screen doors
against my hand and face
every day

ALL THESE HANDS ARE TREE TRUNKS

I remember looking out at
perfect
summer
days

and this is what I think of
when I return to her
one of my *forevers*
for one of hers.

Fairytales and summer
forevers and campfires
and love baby love.

chemical blood

1. All these hands are tree trunks
chest tubes and shoulder valves.

2. There is more to this place
than Marco Polo.
Though I haven't yet learned who is who
I'm memorizing how everyone sleeps
this or that bad dream
at a time.

I see them in the hallways
buckets of scar tissue
beneath their eyelids

I make tallies
always
brow broken bodies and artificial limbs

always
only stopping when my pockets are too full of marbles.

ALL THESE HANDS ARE TREE TRUNKS

Because then all I can think about is marbles.

Also boots that would look good in the rain.
I think about wet leather.

I wonder how all these people
would feel about me if it were raining.
Perhaps they would ask me
if I've ever been in love.
I would tell them my name
like a puzzle
and see how long it takes
before they try and fix me.

3. There is a church of chainsaw silence
at the end of the dinner table.
At the the other end is a house in the round
with the butterfly doors
that swing in   and   out.
In between these there is nothing but
bee sting tongues and rabid dog lips.
And plastic depositions.

This is what I mean by
stop and go motion.

I sit there in between them.

I sit there in between them

and I drink to horses.

I drink kites shaped like biplanes.

I sit there and drink to chalkboards

with hand prints of every size

that are surprisingly hard to wash away.

I drink to the way that feels.

I tell the mismatched flashbulbs

at both ends

what I dreamed of the night before

using my fork and my knife

for dramatic effect.

But I can tell

there is already enough chemical blood

and fire spit sweat

between the house and the church

that I don't bother asking them

what they dream of.

I figure it's either too much to hear

or not enough to hold on to.

I stand up and crack the window.
Then we all smile.

ALL THESE HANDS ARE TREE TRUNKS

I assume we are all thinking about
window-broken summers

or perhaps the way that screen doors smell.

4. There are initials in your concrete bones.
My initials.
It is my system of backseat sainthood.

It has to do with film strips
and photo booths
strobe lights and fish hooks.

Stop and go motion.

I figure if I am written
along the cracks of your body
that there will be enough breaking
for the both of us.

Between my steel breastplate
and flashbang arteries
and your smoke stack fingers
and diamond mine palms

all we would need is that
extra bit of tongue spiral cartilage

around our spines
to keep us upright

and we would call it a day

and a night

and a day.

And then I would ask you what you dreamed about.

5. All these hands are tree trunks
spy-novel romance and bread crumbs.

ALL THESE HANDS ARE TREE TRUNKS

willow trees

when we were kids
we dug holes in the sand
and buried our clothes
everything but our underwear

willow tree wedding vows and pinecone babies
tall grass sanctuaries
and trees for our grandchildren to see

we were in love 77 days of the year
more or less depending on the weather

the rest we were in school
and that made us wise

and in our wisdom
we learned that I was too strange
and you were too pretty

that's when love became willow trees again

Garrett Sherwood

chimes

there are wind chimes
hanging from the slanted gazebo
still in the arms of an avocado tree

at 2:37 pm on september second
there is a moment when the sun peeks through

someone tied a hammock meant for two
to the place the wood slanted most

and when it swung
the avocados rocked
and the chimes danced
and celebrated

darleen

Her name was Darleen and she was careful with her stories.

The busses were full of stories with jagged edges. Strangers telling strangers of halfdreamed *where I come from*s and *you know what I like best about the Midwest…*

At the bus changing station in Idaho Falls in a room attached to a gas station with the intention of imitating somewhere that made sense Darleen had been sitting since the last bus dropped her off, waiting for the next bus to come.

She overheard two men near her telling stories. One was somewhat older and the other quite young but with a beard that seemed to grow only to hide his youngness. The older one was saying *Here are THE top ten strip clubs in the Midwest from number ten to number one. Number ten… Kid you're going to want to write this down.*

He did not write them down.

The room smelled like sweat. Cold sweat. The kind Darleen recognized as a byproduct of shoveling Montana snow, or in this case Idaho snow.

Number seven: East St. Louis. Now, I know what you are thinking...

She thought of the line at the soup kitchen she volunteered at once. Even though they didn't say it, everybody had the same questions sourpunched up behind their eyes as they looked, or rather tried not to look, at each other. *How did you get here? How much longer will this last?*

And like the soup kitchen, here in the bus changing station it was just easier to tell stories.

Number 3: Sioux City. They got this bar, the whole back wall revolves and the whole damn place transforms into a... Hey I think our bus is here.

The switchblade blackness of the greyhound at 2am is the only mask for the dreams everyone carried as their head bobbed between sleep and desperation. The lights from oncoming traffic made the faces flicker.

She noticed youngbeard chose not to sit with his storytelling counterpart but instead sat near the back just across from her against the window. He will never learn about the best strip club in the midwest, she thought. Or maybe that's the point. Or perhaps he just wanted to sit by the window. She had just wanted to sit by the window. This made her smile.

ALL THESE HANDS ARE TREE TRUNKS

Her smile made her feel easy, just enough to let herself close her eyes and rest her head against the vibrational glass, the occasional oncoming headlight flashing red behind the wall of her shut eyelids. She rested.

By the time they reached Denver the bus was blizzard blasted, turned more revolving door of survivors than a throughway. Most had changed their connection in Salt Lake City or had otherwise reached their destination. The only one Darleen recognized any more was youngbeard.

Because of the snow it had been 24 hours since Idaho already. They had missed their connection in Denver. It was night again. No respite until morning.

Darleen sat in a red plastic chair that was captive in a row of 4 other red plastic chairs near the double sliding glass doors to the street. The storms had passed.

The bus terminal became a deserted island. It was full of plane crash victims washed up to shore. She thought it was strange that almost nobody left except for a smoke. It was 2 am. But there seemed to be more world outside than in.

She stood up to leave but her legs couldn't bear the march. How odd, she thought. The place she had never been, that was built more like a prison than a reception parlor, and in no way resembled any sort of place that could be confused as accommodating, felt as much like home as the place she was coming from and the place she was going.

Perhaps everybody was feeling the same thing, she thought.

The entire crowd of strangers, as if all at once exhaling together, began to make beds on the dirty tile floor. They would pass the night as comfortable people do.

Darleen wondered how best to make her bed as well. Youngbeard walked towards her out of the crowd as if they had parted for him. It reminded her of Moses.

Would you watch my bag?

It was the first time she had heard his voice. He asked it in the same way you would ask an old friend. *I guess we are probably more family than anyone else here*, she thought.

Sure. Where are you going?

Out. I read that there is supposed to be a Lunar Eclipse tonight. The moon is red.

Red, she thought. *Red*. She had never seen that. She wanted to ask him where he was really going, not just that night but the next day and the day after that, but she doubted she would get an answer as honest as his first.

ALL THESE HANDS ARE TREE TRUNKS

Not because he was a liar, but because she felt they had an unspeakable trust.

She would never ask him where he was going because she knew he would never ask her.

Will you tell me about it when you get back?

All the way to the Midwest if you'd like.

The man walked out into the red tinted street and looked up.

Darleen looked down at his bag. She closed her eyes. She smiled. And she rested.

Garrett Sherwood

dominoes

you fell on me
just as I was getting ready
to dream again

ALL THESE HANDS ARE TREE TRUNKS

she asked me to write something in the desert

In the elbows of spanish colorful
the moon casts shadows
long and thin
delicate beings
lovers
on the crest of the hill top
three hilltops away from this one.

The truck drivers on the road below
are drowned behind their headlights
shaving off new galaxies
in the neck between the desert air
and the universe above it.

The lovers take their shoes off
and hum the last song they heard
before they stopped for the night

it was a song about God.

Garrett Sherwood

They haven't dreamed in days
but know
there is magic to be had
tonight.

dinosaurs and stuff part 1

I want this be something special.
Something worth reading to my grandchildren
when they ask me why I never cry. I want to
point them in the direction of their grandmother
and tell them

Children,
I believe in God. She wears him
like a sunrise.
Bold breasted and inescapable. And warm. Really warm.
Children,
notice her feet. They may be small but I once
saw those feet
from across a crowded airport terminal
and I'm still pulling splinters of smiles out of my face
from that day.
Children,
when you find God, you start praying with your hands.
Her hands are bomb shelters.
God is fireworks.
And my tears are for putting out the fires.

Garrett Sherwood

I want this to be something special.
so please

please

forgive me if this sucks.

dinosaurs and stuff part 2

to answer your question
this is what I'm thinking about:

the way you say windowsill
the time we brought donuts to a waterfall
how you only dance when no one is looking
the way you squeal when you see anything fluffy
how you love the worst kinds of candy
how you can't pick a favorite color because you would feel bad for the other colors
the way you looked when you said forever
the day I woke up with you beside me
and
RVs and New York City and Mountains and Oceans and Christmas and Guatemala and Puppies and Movies with Lots of Popcorn and The Biggest Truck Stop in the World and Somewhere in the Middle of Utah Snuggled Up in a Car that's Just Not Big Enough but Still Just Right and Dinosaurs and Stuff and You and You and You

Garrett Sherwood

dinosaurs and stuff part 3

1. When I was six years old I loved two things:
Dinosaurs.
And the girl who sat next to me at school.
She played the piano on the pencilholding divot of her desk.

8. I once told you our love was like dominoes
I didn't mean to make it sound so inevitable.
Like a cigarette in a wishing well
I just happened to have dreamt you
before I burned for you.

3. When I was sixteen
I learned to play the blues.
The first song I ever sang was called
Dust My Broom by Robert Johnson.
I played it on a big black guitar
cause
I thought if I was gonna pick a metaphor
for the hollow spots that love picked out
of my white-boy soul
it might as well be big and black.

ALL THESE HANDS ARE TREE TRUNKS

If I had known back then
that I was not singin bout
some new shiver along my neck bones
but rather just a song a blues singer in the 30s
wrote about his penis,
I would have chosen a bigger
blacker
guitar.

4. When I was 26
I found you.
You came to me like a photograph
I kept under my baseball cap
that had you lookin like you owned
the words
lucky boy.

12. See,
it was imagining that someone like you could exist
when I was six years old
that put me in the hole in the first place.
And it was your sunshine hands
and your buttercream gang soul
that have now pulled me out from the windowell.

5. This is a love poem.

7. When your fingers play jazz piano in your sleep
on my stomach
darlin I swear God built you first
in my bone marrow
before he put you in my bed.

2. Fingers have been my favorite part of the female form
since I was 6 years old.

11. My sweet girl,
if I could write a story
about all the punching bag potholes
I bighearted pulled myself out of
it would start and end in with your name.

13. I'm sorry I wrote you a love poem
with the word penis in it.
Twice.

6. But this is not an apology poem.

9. I'm trying to tell you that, baby, you're no accident.

ALL THESE HANDS ARE TREE TRUNKS

15. I just don't always have the words to explain it.

10. That sound you heard when our knees first touched
was the clickin of my bones
stretching from your bottom lip
all the way to the street light above your door step

just tryin to make the moment last
a little bit longer.

14. I love you like six year olds love dinosaurs,
simply
and fearlessly fearlessly fearlessly.

16. Don't you ever take your finger off
the go button.
It's still morning
and we have miles yet to wander.

Garrett Sherwood

the fixer

once a day she takes something apart so that I can put it back together. in this way we can both be sure that there is more to this thing than curlin up good and hot when the train breaks down.

a sock monkey in my windowsill

He sits next to the lousy paper cranes we tried to make one night. an emblem of our ability to make nothing out of something. It's one of the reasons we fell so fast.

Close by is a bamboo plant we bought together during a vegetation purchasing spree, with the agreement that the bamboo would be under my care, as it is the easiest to take care of. It's turned white because I don't know what the hell I'm doing.

I'm laying on a bed built for two thinking about my body as an art studio again, wondering if it changes anything now that someone sees me naked everyday. Probably. And yet it still weirds me out if that sock monkey sees my dingaling.

the end

In the end there will be baskets.
Baskets to hold stuff in.
Because in the end
seems like there's
gonna be a lot stuff scattered.
A lotta stuff we used to hang
sacred from our clothespin lips
but that will
in the end
dance naked in the spider webs
we can only barely see after we
fall face first into them.
Only
our hands won't be so strong in the end
so we're gonna need baskets.

In the end there's gonna be a lot of
restless leg syndrome.
And it won't be as fun as it sounds.

In the end the only cookies will be fig bars
that taste like dollar stores and expletives.

ALL THESE HANDS ARE TREE TRUNKS

In the end
all the poets will still have their heads
and their hearts making love in their throats
trying to get the answers out
in backstabbing monotones.
Only in the end
the questions will be arranged
by relativity and fugues
not by what you can see
but by what you can prove.

In the end no one will be impressed
by metaphors anymore.

In the end the only songs will be
drinking songs
and the only dances will be in long lines
where everybody holds hands
and takes slow sips of the same
burnt out and broken dream whiskey
until all the people start passing out
one on top of the other
making romantic saliva waterfalls
that bounce from one face to the next
collecting at the bottom
in pools of wisecracks
and explicit memories about the big city.

Garrett Sherwood

In the end all dreams
will be about freight trains
impossibly long and fast freight trains
that carry alphabetic love stories
from one town to the next.
Your love stories.
My love stories.
Filed neatly together
at 100 miles per hour
on smooth straight track
passing by just barely too fast
to catch up with
before our eyes split big wide and lonely.

In the end love will be determined
when I grab onto your wrists
with my thumbs over your veins
checking for pulses
counting them
comparing them to mine
being sure you're alive
and then saying
baby it ain't too late
not just yet anyway.

In the end our knuckles will constantly crackle
from clenching too hard.

ALL THESE HANDS ARE TREE TRUNKS

In the end our feet will be dinosaured
from all the broken hearts and bramble
we walk on
and every child's favorite color will be gray
because it's everything
and it's nothing
but mostly because it's just lazy
and there will be no secrets
except for the little secret things
that make you smile

like accidental broken glass art
like the first raindrop on the back of your neck
like the way some people hold their soup spoons
all funny.

No
in the end you'll probably keep those things to yourself.
Sweaty vested
basket handed
and to yourself.

Garrett Sherwood

new lacquer on an old hope chest

I'm feeling pawnshop beautiful
plucked from the afterthought
sitting upright and outbound
mixing fireworks and tonic water

a chinese new year

baby I was born in the year of the tiger

ALL THESE HANDS ARE TREE TRUNKS

Garrett Sherwood

Thank you to...

Matthew Clark for being the Jolly Baba.
Kenneth Guy Richey for the "strawberry moon".
Keith McKenna for being the Smart One.
The Greyhound bus system.
Baldassare Forrestiere for his decision to never stop digging.
Alan for being the bravest man I ever met/imagined.
And all the other half-dreamed but still real-life characters that populated my thoughts and filled these pages.

Also Josh Foster for telling me once that I was a good writer. At least I think he said that.

And Ryan Hayes, even though he told me not to waste my time on poetry.

And my mom and dad for being a spectacular mom and dad.

And Sal and Jay for the endless furry joy they bring.

And of course my dear Brittany. Dominoes, baby, dominoes.

ALL THESE HANDS ARE TREE TRUNKS

About the author and the book

This book, the follow up to my first effort, *Trust Falls Into Wet Cement*, is not just a simple collection of poetry to me. It's a half-dreamed, half-remembered story with lots of characters, some twists and turns, capped off with the happiest of endings. It's a love story at its core, an exploration of love itself as it has fizzled in and out of my oft corrupted vessel, but finally being captured for time and all eternity. This book represents the biggest personal transition of my life, and whether or not it makes an enjoyable read, I hope at least its compassable value is received.

I am a resident of Salt Lake City, Utah. I'm a writer, musician, composer, and a poetry slam contributor, competitor, and supporter. Follow me for all the newest things I do.

garrettsherwood.blogspot.com
facebook.com/sherwood.writes

Garrett Sherwood

www.ingramcontent.com/pod-product-compliance
Lightning Source LLC
Chambersburg PA
CBHW020934090426
42736CB00010B/1129